The First Spam: The Email, Not The Meat

Copyright © by Lon S. Safko, Innovative Thinking, L.L.C.

All rights reserved. No part of this book may be used or reproduced by any means, graphic, electronic, or mechanical, including photocopying, recording, taping or by any information storage retrieval system without the written permission of the publisher except in the case of brief quotations embodied in critical articles and reviews.

Printed in the United States of America

This book was created using 100% recycled electrons

No animals were harmed in the making of this book

This book is dolphin safe

The First Spam: The Email, Not The Meat

Spam Is Inconsistent

Introduction

Over the past several years, there have been a half-dozen reports on the amount of advertising we are subjected to each day. These numbers range from between 3,000 to 20,000 intrusions every day. The reports refer to them as "advertisements" but we know and label them as Spam, junk mail, marketing calls, solicitors, unwanted faxes, billboards, ads, commercials,

The First Spam: The Email, Not The Meat

intrusions, annoyances, aggravation, frustration; or what the FCC in the 2004 CAN-SPAM ACT, calls "Unsolicited Commercial Messages". This book shows us how we look at the different types of spam, our tolerance and penalty for each and asks the question, why is our tolerance for Spam so different for each of the ways it's delivered.

In Part II you are introduced to Gary Thuerk, "The Father of Spam". Yep, you knew someone had to have sent the very first email Spam message and Gary Thuerk is its originator. Gary is the man history recognizes as the one who sent the very first "Spam" email message. It was 40 years ago on May 12, 1978, while working with DARPA. DARPA developed the world's first Internet and email. Gary will tell his story about that event and you will get to read the very first Spam email ever sent.

Gary also shares HOW Spam got its name.

In Part III, Gary shares the actual, first "Unsolicited Commercial Email Message", Spam.

I hope you enjoy!

Lon

PART I

Spam Is Inconsistent
Different Spam, Different Rules

Last evening my cell phone rang during dinner, which is unusual as I mostly use it for business. Since business hours on both coasts were closed for the day. Immediately after my salutation, I realized I was captured by a telemarketer. How did they acquire my cell phone number making it possible to solicit to me during dinner?

I had time to think about it during her long winded and well rehearsed "schpeel"*. I had been out of the office for most of the day and placed my office phone on forward to my cell phone. For a moment I felt relieved because I really didn't want to start getting telemarketers continuously trying to sell me their stuff on my cell.

At about halfway through her pitch, I broke into my speech that makes my wife's eyes roll and causes her to remind me that I will definitely do time in hell for. I ask the telemarketer "What exactly do you tell your spouse and children that you do for a living? Do you tell them you're telemarketer? That your job is to deliberately call 100's of random people a day, people that you don't know, to annoy and upset their dinner, asking them to buy something so some company can make a financial gain for them and yourself? Or, do you have something made up that makes you feel better about what you do and who you are and keeps them from crying? I doubt you tell them the truth that you solicit for money."

As if that wasn't enough, I usually continue by asking them "How do you feel about yourself at the end of each day?" and "Wouldn't you feel better about yourself if you found a different career, any career?" I really do know these are issues I should be working out with a psychiatrist, but I justify it as my way of getting some form of retribution for the incessant inconvenience.

If we could stop this type of telemarketing would we? Of course, we would... And we try. We have the Federal Trade Commission, FTC's "No Call List", or The National Do Not Call Registry (https://www.donotcall.gov/). At least for landline telephones, or does it work for cell phones also? Actually, it does. Go ahead, register your cell phone. I'll wait here.

A Yankelovich Research report quoted by the NY Times (http://nyti.ms/SLMZZP), stated the number of marketing messages the average person is exposed to in any given day is in the range of 3,000 to 20,000 advertisements. What if we could stop all of this. Stop all telemarketers everywhere? What if we could stop all unsolicited advertising? What a perfect world it would be.

Wait a minute… Did I call it "unsolicited advertising"? That's exactly what the FTC called Spam email messages in their CAN SPAM ACT of 2003 or Controlling the Assault of Non-Solicited Pornography And Marketing Act of 2003". In this Federal act, anyone sending an "Unsolicited Commercial Message" via email, if prosecuted can be fined up to $2m for each email. That isn't per email blast, but for each individual email sent. This is why after January 1, 2004, we saw such a dramatic drop in Spam email messages.

Note: The reason we didn't see email Spam go away was that on January 1, 2004, all of the major Spammers, just moved their servers "off-shore" beyond the reach of the FTC.

This got me thinking. How do we define and control commercial messages in all of our other forms of electronic and traditional medias?

The telephone fax is protected against unsolicited commercial faxes through The Federal "Junk Fax Law" or The Telephone Consumer Protection Act of 1991 (http://bit.ly/1Y2quR). This is yet another one of the FTC's toughest laws. I personally met someone who was sued and lost $50,000 in damages even though he never actually sent the fax in question. It was his securities company they ent out a fax blast announcing the sale of his company's stock.

Snail Mail "Junk Mail" was the original unsolicited commercial message we all get every day. Thank goodness for recycling otherwise each year we would send an entire forest to the landfill. How can we control this form of Spam? Can we fine theses marketers as well? Did we "op-in" for junk mail? Can we "opt-out"?

Actually, you can "op-out" according to the USPS (http://1.usa.gov/11Yl9YM). You may go to their Opt-in/opt-out web site (https://www.optoutprescreen.com/) or you can call

1-888-5-OPTOUT (1-888-567-8688). If you receive sexually oriented or obscene mail, you can file PS Form 1500 (http://1.usa.gov/onYPdu) at a local Post Office to prevent or stop the receipt of unwanted obscene materials in the mail.

To stop mail from common mailing lists, the USPS suggests that you "try" contacting The Consumer Credit Reporting Industry's Opt-In/Opt-Out line, which allows you to opt-out for five years, opt-out for life, or opt-in if you change your mind (https://www.optoutprescreen.com/) or you call 1-888-5-OPTOUT (1-888-567-8688).

No fines, possibly some relief, and maybe for "life"!

Then there's the commercial traditional media; television, radio, newspapers, and magazines. Why don't we fine them? Why isn't there any control whatsoever in these medias? Wow, what if we could actually fine marketers who interrupt our television shows, music, and print stories? Did you realize that you only get 22 minutes of your show for every half hour of programming on commercial television? That 16 minutes of advertising for every hour of television you watch. Again, this is controlled by the FTC and the FCC.

If you are a baby-boomer, then you remember the cable TV company's schpeel that if you paid for their television each month, you would get commercial free television forever! It's "like paying up front so you don't have to pay with continuous commercial interruptions". How did that work out for us? Still no fines and no control.

Radio also has the same FTC / FCC guidelines as they have for television, limiting the number of and overall airtime per hour airing their Spam messages.

Newspapers choose their own limits on Spam or advertisements. And, magazines like newspapers self-control their amount of Spam. Has anyone noticed that this self-imposed limit is getting significantly worse? Both newspapers and magazines seem to be out-of-control as to the number of column inches used for Spam often exceed the actual column inches of content!

Can we ever control these medias forms of Spam? Should we? Why do we completely tolerate Spam in our television, radio, newspapers, and magazines, but heavily fine people for the exact same advertisement in email or over a fax? Is there a distinction between an "unsolicited commercial message" and an "anticipated commercial message"? Are television, radio, and print "anticipated" not "unsolicited"? It certainly is not "solicited".

This leads us to social media marketing. How do we treat Spam in our social spaces? The short answer is "with very little tolerance!" If you try to "sell" on Facebook, LinkedIn, or Twitter, you get "flamed" or "blocked". Offended people will let you know it. There are no fines or penalties on these networks; however, people will "unlink", "unfollow", "unfriend", "unsubscribe", and "opt-out" of your relationship communication.

Why don't we impose such huge fines on "unsolicited commercial messages" in all of our media? Why are the rules inconsistent with controlling Spam everywhere? Why do some media get preferential treatment while others get slammed with fines? What if the same rules applied to television, radio, magazines, and newspapers that applies to email marketing, wouldn't that usher in the end of all marketing and advertising as we know it?

The First Spam: The Email, Not The Meat

So, where is the appropriate line in marketing? When IS it appropriate to pass on our unsolicited marketing messages? Where should the line be and should it be completely different for every technology and every media? Somehow, it just doesn't seem fair or equitable. What are your thoughts?

*Urban Dictionary (http://bit.ly/haszKl) defines "Shpeel" as

"Oft-repeated thoughtless dialogue which is not necessarily true."

PART II

The First Spam Email Message Sent

Gary Thuerk had been working at Digital Equipment Corporation (DEC) for over a year in 1977 when he was promoted to DoD (Department of Defense) Marketing Manager. One morning, while passing John Lang, V.P. of the Large Computer System Division for DEC, in the hall, he stopped Gary and asked if DEC had done a lot of business with the ARPA community. In previous years, ARPA* had bought a lot of DEC KA-10s in the past but hadn't purchased any in recent years. He asked Gary to check them out.

*Note: The Defense Advanced Research Projects Agency (DARPA) is an agency of the U.S. Department of Defense responsible for the development of emerging technologies for use by the military.

Originally known as the Advanced Research Projects Agency (ARPA), the agency was created in February 1958 by

President Dwight D. Eisenhower in response to the Soviet launching of Sputnik 1 in 1957.

Gary had heard of ARPA, but only in passing, so he began marketing to them as if they were a new client in a new market. At this same time, the ARPA agency had changed to DARPA (The Defense Advanced Research Agency.)

His first stop was the DARPA headquarters in Arlington VA. They were located in a medium height modern looking office building with no exterior signage, across the Francis Scott Key Bridge leading to Georgetown, DC. The outside appearance was very minimal. Its appearance would never expose the top secret, futuristic projects that were being developed just inside their doors.

Gary and his manager, Fred Wilhelm then ad the opportunity to meet both Vint Cerf and Robert Kahn, the now recognized "Fathers of the Internet. Sadly, they realized that DARPA HQ did not have a budget to spend on their own computers, but did allocate funds for other projects groups across the country. They were able to obtain an ARPANET directory, listing locations, organizations, and people on the ARPAnet, containing the world's first e-mail addresses.

Throughout the next year, Gary visited many of the ARPANET sites gathering information about their projects and computer needs. He would set up meetings with and without the local DEC sales team, many of whom were unaware of the local projects, as you would expect with customers with no money to spend. Gary would plan to visit the DARPA contractor sites as part of his regular marketing trips and in support of the DEC sales force.

The DARPA sites around Washington D.C. and Boston were easy to visit from his office and he made frequent trips to DC. The sites in the middle of the county and the west coast were harder to contact and therefore seldom met with.

The First Spam: The Email, Not The Meat

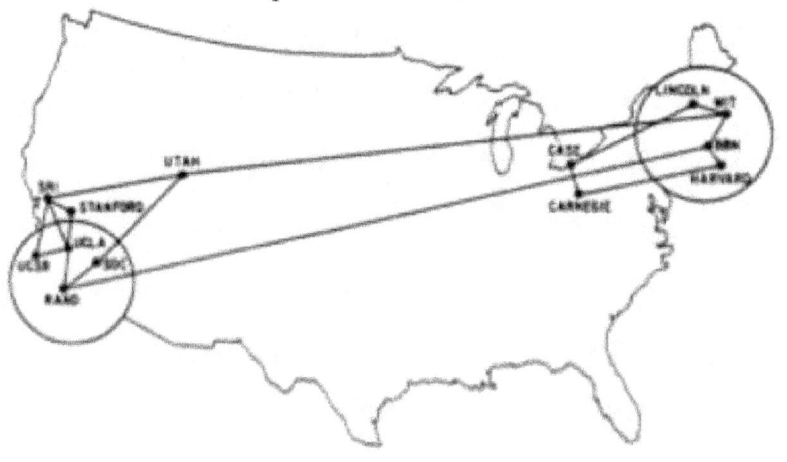

The Early ARPANET Map - Circa 1970

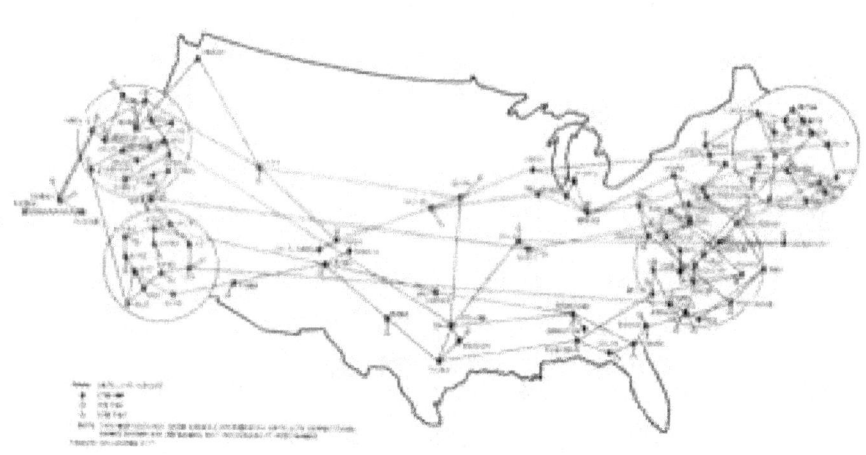

The Early ARPANET Map - Circa 1984

Email & file transfer were the 2 main applications the developers used to collaborate and invent the functionality everyone takes for granted today. About this time, the developers were working on the first local area networks (LANs), to extend the reach of the ARPANET backbone.

Ringnet and Ethernet were the 2 competing technologies at this time.

The Ringnet LAN would have every information packet going in one direction around a circle (or ring), with a point of central control, while the Ethernet LAN would have its packets go in both directions (or either-way).

Both groups claimed that their LAN technology was superior to one another's. So, DAPRA HQ funded a LAN test bed at MIT to test both competing LANs. MIT had one of the first AI (artificial intelligence) labs at the time. Down the hall and in keeping with the usual MIT sense of humor, a sign on the door read "Real Intelligence Lab".

The AI Lab wired both and compared their performance. They found that at the low & medium usage volumes both performed equally as well, but when the systems were stressed with high volumes of data packets there were large differences. The ring-net would experience delays when overloaded and the Ethernet would not see the same slowdown. It actually produced a self-generated heartbeat the seemed to make everything work better together.

Returning from a business trip from the west coast DARPA contractors, he suddenly realized each of the user sites had to custom build their own network hardware to connect to every individual computer to the ARPAnet IMP. The IMP Being The Interface Message Processor.

They would need to write the software protocols for every type and model of computer to support the packet switching IMP interface along with what was called the 1822 protocol code. This is when he got the idea to have their new DECsystem-10 and DECsystem-20 support the ARPAnet. This thinking was a game-changing idea for its time.

Gary approached his V.P. John Lang, with the proposition of supporting the new ARPAnet's 1822 protocol and necessary IMP Hardware interface. He instructed Gary to his design into a one-page business plan and estimate the minimum number of units they could sell. Upon completion of the plan, he estimated they would sell a minimum of 12 DEC-systems, each price from $800k to $1.2 million ($3,215,881 to $$4,823,821 in today's dollars!)

The development process started with the DEC Large Computer Group Engineering, designing and building the IMP interface box along with DEC's software engineers rewriting all the code necessary to meet the then commercial standards. They did this through close collaboration with the ARPAnet developers who were very interested in a standard product with much higher performance than their current time-share systems. To bring it back in your mind, it was 1977 and the first Star Wars movie was showing in movie theaters.

The First Spam: The Email, Not The Meat

The DECsystem-1080 - Circa 1978

The DECsystem-2060 - Circa 1978

Carl Gartley was assigned to Gary as the product manager on this new DEC venture. Carl divided his time between Gary in Marketing, Hardware engineering, software development, and eventually the system testing center. Their development team interacted with the ARPAnet development teams throughout the product development and test stages.

Once underway, it was time to get the word out about the first commercially available computer to support packet-switching on the ARPAnet. Excited, Gary wanted to do a product announcement and demo to get the ARPA communities attention.

The DEC Team still had the problem of reaching ARPAnet's users and their individual sites. Gary knew these people seldom answered their office telephones, he had been trying that for over a year. They thought about mailing invitations, but he had already begged for money just to print the product brochure.

That was the eureka moment. They became inspired with the idea to send out the invitations via email. This would be the first time

The First Spam: The Email, Not The Meat

anyone would use the primitive ARPAnet to communicate a commercial message -Spam!

Gary took the "ARPANET Directory" and highlighted about 400 names of users (sites) in the most western U.S. states. They then arranged the hotel and flight reservations for the west coast demos.

Carl took the highlighted ARPANET Directory and started entering the names & email addresses (see the original email attached below). Gary typed up the invitation text all in uppercase characters so it would appear more formal. They only had what today is called "text-doc lettering", there were no WYSIWYG (What You See Is What You Get).

Then on May 3rd, 1978, they hit the "return key" and sent the first email-spam. Keep in mind, the term "spam", an unsolicited mass commercial email hadn't yet been invented.

Within only 3 to 4 days they started hearing the complaints. Oddly enough, the complaints were not about getting the unsolicited email, it was that they had not made a "distribution list". As a result, the number of addressees overloaded the system and pushed many of the addresses into the email body itself. (also see below).

The second, lesser complaint was that he typed it all in capital letters. At that time, everyone thought Gary was "shouting" at them. How was he to know? There were no official rules of etiquette yet.

As the email spread, many were happy to receive the good news.

But, then came the big surprise. Gary's manager Fred Wilhelm, (remember him?), received an irate phone call from the Defense Communication Agency, DCA who now was responsible for the operational management of the ARPAnet. It was an Air Force Major who chewed out Fred and Gary both for using the ARPAnet to send out their unsolicited commercial email message trying to sell commercial DEC products, even though it was to everyone on the ARPAnet, advantage.

Gary also got an irate personal email from a guy at the Rand Corporation in southern California, taking him to task for the commercial use of the ARPAnet. He felt that Gary's email endangered access and his use of the ARPAnet was inappropriate for anyone who was considered a non-military type. (Gary really wishes he had a copy of that email reply so he could try to contact him.)

The Show Must Go On

Soon, Fred Wilhelm and Gary were flying off to LAX, where they had shipped their first DECsystem-2020 ahead of them for use in their demonstrations. The first demo was arranged and launched with all of the usual dial-up phone problems.

There were about 20± attendees at each of the demonstrations.

Several of the attendees had the opportunity to work on the new DECsystem-2020 to test their ARPAnet functionality. The new systems worked as advertised and everyone was impressed!

Gary sold much more than the 12 DEC systems he had originally promised in his one-page business plan. The DARPA customers purchased between 40 to 50 DEC system-T's with the support of ARPAnet over the life of the product.

The DECsystem-2020 - Circa 1979

The DEC VAX computers were connecting to the Internet weekly before most people even heard the term "Internet."

The next step they saw was the need for the LAN to extend the packet network around a campus or building complex. Aware of how the LAN development worked, they decided to seek approval to develop a Ringnet product. They estimated that it should only take about 6 months since they already had the packet-switching 1822 protocol working. At the very same, time

SRI International was also working on a wireless LAN protocol (think Wi-Fi.) Really...

Their Ringnet proposal was subsequently turned down without an explanation. Later they found out that DEC was working together with HP, Intel, and Xerox-PARK (Palo Alto Research Center), on a shared development of the commercial Ethernet LAN products. The first DEC Ethernet LAN controller consisted of 3 circuit boards with a connection to coaxial cable and sold for about $8k ($32,158.81 in today's dollars.)

Three years later, Gary was called to take responsibility for the AT&T ACS packet-switching opportunity, which was in early its early development stages.

And, as they say... The Rest Is History. Well Almost.

How Spam Actually Got Its Name

There is one additional piece of information Gary has shared about the history of email Spam, how it got its name.

To understand email Spam, you must first understand the original product with that name.

"The term SPAM originally comes from the meat produced by the Hormel Meat Packing Company in Austin, Minnesota, in 1937. Then-president J. C. Hormel created an amazing little recipe: a spicy ham packaged in a handy 12-ounce can. He held a contest to give the product a name as distinctive as its taste. The winner was SPAM, for **SP**iced h**AM**. During its very first year of production, SPAM grabbed 18 percent of the market. Seven billion cans of SPAM have been sold since 1937, with 44,000 cans per hour rolling out of Hormel. A can of SPAM is consumed in the United States every 3.1 seconds.

How does this translate to online clutter, though? Well, when it comes to the Internet, you've likely seen, heard, or even used the term spam and spamming, which refers to the act of sending unsolicited commercial e-mail (UCE), which implies that someone has sent a message that has no value or substance inside for the recipient.

How might a company feel about its product being likened to something without value or substance? Hormel's official position on the term spam is as follows: "We do not object to use of this slang term to describe UCE, although we do object to the use of the word 'spam' as a trademark and to the use of our product image in association with that term. Also, if the term is to be used, it should be used in all lower-case letters to distinguish it from our trademark SPAM, which should be used with all upper-case letters."

Excerpt from Chapter 5 of "The Social Media Bible", published by John Wiley & Sons. Available on Amazon in both eBook and Paperback.

I was familiar with this side of the story and the connection between the email and the meat, but I wanted to know how it got called Spam, so I asked Gary that very question.

He told me although he wasn't personally involved. The story of how "spam" became the name of unsolicited mass commercial email, because he was traveling in those circles when it happened.

It came from The BBC show Monty Python's Flying Circus who was famous for their memorable "Spam" sketch first televised in 1970.

The skit takes place in a pub during breakfast, as an old married couple played by Eric Idle as Mr. Bun and Graham Chapman as Mrs. Bun are lowered in from the ceiling above into two waiting chairs where Terry Jones plays the Waitress. The viewer will also take-note the entire cafe is filled with "Viking" patrons. The original sketch also featured John Cleese as
The Hungarian and Michael Palin as a historian.

As the waitress reads the menu to Mrs. Bun, nearly every item contains SPAM, Mrs. Bun keeps insisting that she doesn't like or want any SPAM. As the Waitress reads down the menu, every item contains increasingly more SPAM. The husband suggested his favorite SPAM meal, as the Wife shouts SPAM, SPAM, SPAM, I HATE SPAM ! ! !

Here's link where you can watch that iconic sketch on YouTube: http://bit.ly/1knsQUA

The First Spam: The Email, Not The Meat

Eight years later a computer techy, who had watched a re-run of this Monty Python's episode was confronted at work with his email inbox filled with unsolicited commercial email messages. Out of complete frustration, he shouted – "SPAM, SPAM, SPAM, I HATE SPAM ! ! !"

To his fellow computer techy's in the room, his tantrum and mantra seemed so appropriate the term Spam quickly spread throughout the development team and eventually the world.

PART III

As promised, here is the world's first "Unsolicited Commercial EMail Message" or Spam.

The Actual First Spam Email Sent, In Its Entirety

Note 1: *There were too many email addresses for the server to handle which caused them to spill over into the body of the email.*

The First Spam: The Email, Not The Meat

Mail-from DEC-MARLBORO rcvd at 3-May-78 0955-PDT
Date: 1 May 1978 1233-EDT
From THUERK at DEC-MARLBORO
Subject: ADRIAN@SRI-KL
To: DDAY at SRI-KL, DAY at SRI-KL, DEBOER at UCLA-CCN,
To: WASHDC at SRI-KL, LOGICON at USC-ISI, SDAC at USC-ISI,
To: DELDO at USC-ISI, DELEOT at USC-ISI, DELFINO at USC-ISI,
To: DENCOFF at USC-ISI, DESPAIN at USC-ISI, DEUTSCH at SRI-KL,
To: DEUTSCH at PARC-MAXC, EMY at CCA-TENEX, DIETER at USC-ISIB,
To: DINES at AMES-67, MERADCON at SRI-KL, EPG-SPEC at SRI-KA,
To: DIVELY at SRI-KL, DODD at USC-ISI, DONCHIN at USC-ISIC,
To: JED at LLL-COMP, DORIN at CCA-TENEX, NYU at SRI-KA,
To: DOUGHERTY at USC-ISI, PACOMJ6 at USC-ISI,
To: DEBBY at UCLA-SECURITY, BELL at SRI-KL, JHANNON at SRI-KA,
To: DUBOIS at USC-ISI, DUDA at SRI-KL, POH at USC-ISI,
To: LES at SU-AI, EAST at BBN-TENEX, DEASTMAN at USC-ECL,
To: EBISU at I4-TENEX, NAC at USC-ISIE, ECONOMIDIS at I4-TENEX,
To: WALSH at SRI-KL, GEDWARDS at SRI-KL, WEDWARDS at USC-ISI,

To: NUSC at SRI-KL, RM at SU-AI, ELKIND at PARC-MAXC,
To: ELLENBY at PARC-MAXC, ELLIS at PARC-MAXC, ELLIS at USC-ISIB,
To: ENGELBART at SRI-KL, ENGELMORE at SUMEX-AIM,
To: ENGLISH at PARC-MAXC, ERNST at I4-TENEX,
To: ESTRIN at MIT-MULTICS, EYRES at USC-ISIC,
To: FAGAN at SUMEX-AIM, FALCONER at SRI-KL,
To: DUF at UCLA-SECURITY, FARBER at RAND-UNIX, PMF at SU-AI,
To: HALFF at USC-ISI, RJF at MIT-MC, FEIERBACH at I4-TENEX,
To: FEIGENBAUM at USC-ISI, FEINLER at SRI-KL,
To: FELDMAN at SUMEX-AIM, FELDMAN at SRI-KL, FERNBACH at LLL-COMP,
To: FERRARA at RADC-MULTICS, FERRETTI at SRI-KA,
To: FIALA at PARC-MAXC, FICKAS at USC-ISIC, AFIELD at I4-TENEX,
To: FIKES at PARC-MAXC, REF at SU-AI, FINK at MIT-MULTICS,
To: FINKEL at USC-ISIB, FINN at USC-ISIB, AFGWC at BBN-TENEX,
To: FLINT at SRI-KL, WALSH at SRI-KL, DRXAN at SRI-KA,
To: FOX at SRI-KL, FRANCESCHIN at MIT-MULTICS,
To: SAI at USC-ISIC, FREDRICKSON at RAND-RCC, ETAC at BBN-TENEXB,
To: FREYLING at BBN-TENEXE, FRIEDLAND at SUMEX-AIM,

The First Spam: The Email, Not The Meat

To: FRIENDSHUH at SUMEX-AIM, FRITSCH at LLL-COMP, ME at SU-AI,

To: FURST at BBN-TENEXB, FUSS at LLL-COMP, OP-FYE at USC-ISIB,

To: SCHLL at USC-ISIC, GAGLIARDI at USC-ISIC,

To: GAINES at RAND-UNIX, GALLENSON at USC-ISIB,

To: GAMBLE at BBN-TENEXE, GAMMILL at RAND-UNIX,

To: GANAN at USC-ISI, GARCIA at SUMEX-AIM,

To: GARDNER at SUMEX-AIM, MCCUTCHEN at SRI-KL,

To: GARDNER at MIT-MULTICS, GARLICK at SRI-KL,

To: GARVEY at SRI-KL, GAUTHER at USC-ISIB,

To: USGS-LIA at BBN-TENEX, GEMOETS at I4-TENEX,

To: GERHART at USC-ISIB, GERLA at USC-ISIE, GERLACH at I4-TENEX,

To: GERMAN at HARV-10, GERPHEIDE at SRI-KA, DANG at SRI-KL,

To: GESCHKE at PARC-MAXC, GIBBONS at CMU-10A,

To: GIFFORD.COMPSYS at MIT-MULTICS, JGILBERT at BBN-TENEXB,

To: SGILBERT at BBN-TENEXB, SDAC at USC-ISI,

To: GILLOGLY at RAND-UNIX, STEVE at RAND-UNIX,

To: GLEASON at SRI-KL, JAGBIN(1525) at UCLA-CCN,

To: GOLD at LL-11, GOLDBERG at USC-ISIB, GOLDGERG at SRI-KL,

To: GROBSTEIN at SRI-KL, GOLDSTEIN at BBN-TENEXB,

To: DARPM-NW at BBN-TENEXB, GOODENOUGH at USC-ISIB,

To: GEOFF at SRI-KL, GOODRICH at I4-TENEX, GOODWIN at USC-ISI,

To: GOMINSKY at SRI-KL, DEAN at I4-TENEX, TEG at MIT-MULTICS,

To: CCG at SU-AI, EPG-SPEC at SRI-KA, GRISS at USC-ECL,

To: BJG at RAND-UNIX, MCCUTCHEN at SRI-KL, GROBSTEIN at SRI-KL,

To: MOBAH at I4-TENEX, GUSTAFSON at USC-ISIB, GUTHARY at SRI-KL,

To: GUTTAG at USC-ISIB, GUYTON at RAND-RCC,

To: ETAC-AD at BBN-TENEXB, HAGMANN at USC-ECL, HALE at I4-TENEX,

To: HALFF at USC-ISI, DEHALL at MIT-MULTICS,

To: HAMPEL at LLL-COMP, HANNAH at USC-ISI,

To: NORSAR-TIP at USC-ISIC, SCRL at USC-ISI, HAPPY at SRI-KL,

To: HARDY at SRI-KL, IMPACT at SRI-KL, KLH at SRI-KL,

To: J33PAC at USC-ISI, HARRISON at SRI-KL, WALSH at SRI-KL,

To: DRCPM-FF at BBN-TENEXB, HART at AMES-67, HART at SRI-KL,

To: HATHAWAY at AMES-67, AFWL at I4-TENEX, BHR at RAND-UNIX,

To: RICK at RAND-UNIX, DEBE at USC-ISIB, HEARN at USC-ECL,

To: HEATH at UCLA-ATS, HEITMEYER at BBN-TENEX, ADTA at SRI-KA,

To: HENDRIX at SRI-KL, CH47M at BBN-TENEXB, HILLIER at SRI-KL,

The First Spam: The Email, Not The Meat

To: HISS at I4-TENEX, ASLAB at USC-ISIC, HOLG at USC-ISIB,
To: HOLLINGWORTH at USC-ISIB, HOLLOWAY at HARV-10,
To: HOLMES at SRI-KL, HOLSWORTH at SRI-KA, HOLT at LLL-COMP,
To: HOLTHAM at LL, DHOLZMAN at RAND-UNIX, HOPPER at USC-ISIC,
To: HOROWITZ at USC-ISIB, VSC at USC-ISI, HOWARD at LLL-COMP,
To: HOWARD at USC-ISI, PURDUE at USC-ISI, HUBER at RAND-RCC,
To: HUNER at RADC-MULTICS, HUTSON at AMES-67, IMUS at USC-ISI,
To: JACOBS at USC-ISIE, JACOBS at BBN-TENEXB,
To: JACQUES at BBN-TENEXB, JARVIS at PARC-MAXC,
To: JEFFERS at PARC-MAXC, JENKINS at PARC-MAXC,
To: JENSEN at SRI-KA, JIRAK at SUMEX-AIM, NCKIE at SRI-KL,
To: JOHNSON at SUMEX-AIM, JONES at SRI-KL, JONES at LLL-COMP,
To: JONES at I4-TENEX, RLJ at MIT-MC, JURAK at USC-ECL,
To: KAHLER at SUMEX-AIM, MWK at SU-AI, KAINE at USC-ISIB,
To: KALTGRAD at UCLA-ATS, MARK at UCLA-SECURITY, RAK at SU-AI,
To: KASTNER at USC-ISIB, KATT at USC-ISIB,
To: UCLA-MNC at USC-ISI, ALAN at PARC-MAXC, KEENAN at USC-ISI,

To: KEHL at UCLA-CCN, KELLEY at SRI-KL, BANANA at I4-TENEX,
To: KELLOGG at USC-ISI, DDI at USC-ISI, KEMERY at SRI-KL,
To: KEMMERER at UCLA-ATS, PARVIZ at UCLA-ATS, KING at SUMEX-AIM,
To: KIRSTEIN at USC-ISI, SDC at UCLA-SECURITY,
To: KLEINROCK at USC-ISI, KLEMBA at SRI-KL, CSK at USC-ISI,
To: KNIGHT at SRI-KL, KNOX at USC-ISI, KODA at USC-ISIB,
To: KODAN at AMES-67, KOOIJ at USC-ISI, KREMERS at SRI-KL,
To: BELL at SRI-KL, KUNZELMAN at SRI-KL, PROJX at SRI-KL,
To: LAMPSON at PARC-MAXC, SDL at RAND-UNIX, JOJO at SRI-KL,
To: SDC at USC-ISI, NELC3030 at USC-ISI,
To: LEDERBERG at SUMEX-AIM, LEDUC at SRI-KL, JSLEE at USC-ECL,
To: JACOBS at USC-ISIE, WREN at USC-ISIB, LEMONS at USC-ISIB,
To: LEUNG at SRI-KL, J33PAC at USC-ISI, LEVIN at USC-ISIB,
To: LEVINTHAL at SUMEX-AIM, LICHTENBERGER at I4-TENEX,
To: LICHTENSTEIN at USC-ISI, LIDDLE at PARC-MAXC,
To: LIEB at USC-ISIB, LIEBERMAN at SRI-KL, STANL at USC-ISIE,
To: LIERE at I4-TENEX, DOCB at USC-ISIC, LINDSAY at SRI-KL,

The First Spam: The Email, Not The Meat

To: LINEBARGER at AMES-67, LIPKIS at USC-ECL, SLES at USC-ISI,

To: LIS at SRI-KL, LONDON at USC-ISIB, J33PAC at USC-ISI,

To: LOPER at SRI-KA, LOUVIGNY at SRI-KL, LOVELACE at USC-ISIB,

To: LUCANIC at SRI-KL, LUCAS at USC-ISIB, DCL at SU-AI,

To: LUDLAM at UCLA-CCN, YNGVAR at SRI-KA, LYNCH at SRI-KL,

To: LYNN at USC-ISIB, MABREY at SRI-KL, MACKAY at AMES-67,

To: MADER at USC-ISIB, MAGILL at SRI-KL, KMAHONEY at BBN-TENEX,

To: MANN at USC-ISIB, ZM at SU-AI, MANNING at USC-ISI,

To: MANTIPLY at I4-TENEX, MARIN at I4-TENEX, SCRL at USC-ISI,

To: HARALD at SRI-KA, GLORIA-JEAN at UCLA-CCN, MARTIN at USC-ISIC,

To: VMARTIN at USC-ISI, GRM at RAND-UNIX, MASINTER at USC-ISI,

To: MASON at USC-ISIB, MATHIS at SRI-KL, MAYNARD at USC-ISIC,

To: MCBREARTY at SRI-KL, MCCALL at SRI-KA, MCCARTHY at SU-AI,

To: MCCLELLAND at USC-ISI, DORIS at RAND-UNIX, MCCLURG at SRI-KL,

To: JOHN at I4-TENEX, MCCREIGHT at PARC-MAXC, MCCRUMB at USC-ISI,

Note 2: *here how we get to the body of the message and there are still addresses going into it that wouldn't fit!*

MCKINLEY@USC-ISIB
MMCM@SRI-KL
OT-ITS@SRI-KA
BELL@SRI-KL
MEADE@SRI-KL
MARTIN@USC-ISI
MERRILL@BBN-TENEX
METCALFE@PARC-MAXC
JMETZGER@USC-ISIB
MICHAEL@USC-ISIC
CMILLER@SUMEX-AIM
MILLER@USC-ISI
SCI@USC-ISI
MILLER@USC-ISIC
MITCHELL@PARC-MAXC
MITCHELL@USC-ISI
MITCHELL@SUMEX-AIM
MLM@SU-AI
JPDG@TENEXB
MOORE@USC-ISIB
WMORE@USC-ISIB
JAM@SU-AI
MORAN@PARC-MAXC
ROZ@SU-AI

MORGAN@USC-ISIB
MORRIS@PARC-MAXC
MORRIS@I4-TENEX
OT-ITS@SRI-KA
LISA@USC-ISIB
MOSHER@SRI-KL
MULHERN@USC-ISI
MUNTZ;BIN(1529)@UCLA-CCN
MYERS@USC-ISIC
MYERS@RAND-RCC
DRCPM-FF-FO@BBN-TENEXB
NAGEL@USC-ISIB
NAPKE@SRI-KL
NARDI@SRI-KL
NAYLOR@USC-ISIE
LOU@USC-ISIE
NESBIT@RAND-RCC
NEUMANN@SRI-KA
NEVATIA@USC-ECL
NEWBY@USC-ISI
NEWEKK@SRI-KA
NIELSON@SRI-KL
NLL@SUMEX-AIM
NILSSON@SRI-KL
NITZAN@SRI-KL
NOEL@USC-ISIC
NORMAN@PARC-MAXC
NORTON@SRI-KL

JOAN@USC-ISIB
NOURSE@SUMEX-AIM
PDG@SRI-KL
OMALLEY@SRI-KA
OCKEN@USC-ISIC
OESTREICHER@USC-ISIB
OGDEN@SRI-KA
OKINAKA@USC-ISIE
OLSON@I4-TENEX
ORNSTEIN@PARC-MAXC
PANKO@SRI-KL
TED@SU-AI
PARK@SRI-KL
PBARAN@USC-ISI
PARKER@USC-ISIB
PEARCE@USC-ISI
PEPIN@USC-ECL
PERKINS@USC-ISIB
PETERS@SRI-KL
AMPETERSON@USC-ISI
ASLAB@USC-ISIC
EPG-SPEC@SRI-KA
PEZDIRTZ@LLL-COMP
CHARLIE@I4-TENEX
UCLA-DOC@USC-ISI
WPHILLIPS@USC-ISI
PIERCY@MOFFETT-ARC

PINE@SRI-KL
PIPES@I4-TENEX
PIRTLE@SRI-KL
POGGIO@USC-ISIC
POH@USC-ISI
POOL@BBN-TENEX
POPEK@USC-ISI
POSTEL@USC-ISIB
POWER@SRI-KL
PRICE@USC-ECL
RANDALL@USC-ISIB
RANDALL@SRI-KA
RAPHAEL@SRI-KL
RAPP@RAND-RCC
RASMUSSEN@USC-ISIC
RATTNER@SRI-KL
RAY@LL-NTX
FNWC@I4-TENEX
BRL@SRI-KL
RETZ@SRI-KL
SKIP@USC-ISIB
RICHARDSON@USC-ISIB
RICHES@USC-ECL
GWEN@USC-ECL
OP-RIEDEL@USC-ISIB
RIES@LL-COMP
RINDFLEISCH@SUMEX-AIM
OP-ROBBINS@USC-ISIB

ROBINSON@SRI-KL
JROBINSON@SRI-KL
RODRIQUEZ@SRI-KL
MARTIN@USC-ISI
ROM@USC-ISIC
ROMEZ@I4-TENEX
ROSE@USC-ISI
ROSEN@SRI-KL
BARBARA@I4-TENEX
ROTHENBERG@USC-ISIB
RUBIN@SRI-KL
JBR@SU-AI
RUBINSTEIN@BBN-TENEXD
RUDY@USC-ECL
RUGGERI@SRI-KA
RULIFSON@PARC-MAXC
DALE@USC-ISIB
SACERDOTI@SRI-KL
SAGALOWICZ@SRI-KL
ALS@SU-AI
SANTON@USC-ISIC
SATTERTHWAITE@PARC-MAXC
SAWCHUK@USC-ECL
CPF-CC@USC-ISI
SCHELONKA@USC-ISI
SCHILL@USC-ISIC
SCHILLING@USC-ISI

SCHULZ@SUMEX-AIM
SCOTT@SUMEX-AIM
CPF-CC@USC-ISI
OP-SEATON@USC-ISIB
SENNE@LL
NORM@RAND-UNIX
AFWL@I4-TENEX
SHEPPARD@LL-ASG
SHERWIN@USC-ISI
SHERWOOD@SRI-KL
SHORT@SRI-KL
SHORTLIFE@SUMEX-AIM
SHOSHANI@BBN-TENEX
MARTIN@USC-ISI
UCLA-NMC@USC-ISIE
SDL@USC-ISIC
SKOCYPEC@USC-ISI
SLES@USC-ISI
SLOTTOW@UCLA-CCN
NOAA@I4-TENEX
SMALL@USC-ISI
DAVESMITH@PARC-MAXC
DSMITH@RAND-UNIX
SMITH@SUMEX-AIM
SMITH@USC-ECL
MARCIE@I4-TENEX
USARSGEUR@USC-ISI
LOGICON@USC-ISI

EPA@SRI-KL
SONDEREGGER@USC-ISIB
SPEER@LL
AMICON-RN@USC-ISI
SPROULL@PARC-MAXC
PROJX@SRI-KL
STEF@SRI-KA
STEFIK@SUMEX-AIM
STEPHENS@SRI-KA
CFD@I4-TENEX
STOCKHAM@SRI-KA
STOTZ@USC-ISIB
ALLEN@UCLA-SECURITY
STOUTE@MIT-ML
STRADLING@SRI-KL
STROLLO@PARC-MAXC
UCLA-0638@UCLA-CCN
CRT@SRI-KA
SUNSHINE@RAND-UNIX
SUTHERLAND@SRI-KL
SUTHERLAND@RAND-UNIX
SUTHERLAND@PARC-MAXC
SUTTON@USC-ISIC
SWEER@SUMEX-AIM
TAFT@PARC-MAXC
TAYLOR@USC-ISIB
TAYLOR@PARC-MAXC

TAYNAI@SUMEX-AIM
TEITELMAN@PARC-MAXC
TENENBAUM@SRI-KL
GREEP@RAND-UNIX
TERRY@SUMEX-AIM
TESLER@PARC-MAXC
THACKER@PARC-MAXC
PWT@RAND-UNIX
TIPPIT@USC-ISIE
TOBAGI@USC-ISIE
TOGNETTI@SUMEX-AIM
TORRES@SRI-KL
TOWNLEY@HARV-10
ELINA@UCLA-ATS
TUCKER@SUMEX-AIM
TUGENDER@USC-ISIB
LLLSRG@MIT-MC
UNCAPHER@USC-ISIB
NOSC@SRI-KL
UNTULIS@SRI-KL
MIKE@UCLA-SECURITY
AARDVARK@UCLA-ATS
UZGALIS.BIN(0836)@UCLA-CCN
VANGOETHEM@UCLA-CCN
VANMIEROP@USC-ISIB
VANNOUHUYS@SRI-KL
VEIZADES@SUMEX-AIM
VESECKY@USC-ISI

AV@MIT-DMS
VICTOR@USC-ISIC
VIDAL@UCLA-SECURITY
OP-VILAIN@USC-ISIB
RV@RAND-UNIX
SDL@USC-ISIC
VOLPE@SRI-KL
VONNEGUT@I4-TENEX
VU@SRI-KL
WACTLAR@CMU-10A
WAGNER@USC-ISI
WAHRMAN@RAND-UNIX
WALDINGER@SRI-KL
WALKER@UCLA-SECURITY
WALKER@SRI-KL
WALLACE@PARC-MAXC
EVE@UCLA-SECURITY
LOGICON@USC-ISI
DON@RAND-UNIX
WATSON@USC-ISIC
WEIDEL@USC-ECL
WEINBERG@SRI-KL
JLW@MIT-AI
LAUREN@UCLA-SECURITY
WEISSMAN@I4-TENEX
WELLS@USC-ISIC
GERSH@USC-ISI

WETHEREL@LLL-COMP
RWW@SU-AI
SCRL@USC-ISI
TWHELLER@SRI-KA
MABREY@SRI-KL
WHITE@PARC-MAXC
WHITE@SUMEX-AIM
WIEDERHOLD@SUMEX-AIM
WILBER@SRI-KL
EPG-SPEC@SRI-KA
WILCOX@SUMEX-AIM
WILCZYNSKI@USC-ISIB
WILE@USC-ISIB
OP-WILLIAMS@USC-ISIB
WILSON@USC-ISIB
TW@SU-AI
SCI@USC-ISI
WISNIEWSKI@RAND-UNIX
WOLF@SRI-KL
PAT@SU-AI
NELC3030@USC-ISI
WYATT@HARV-10
LEO@USC-ISIB
YEH@LLL-COMP
YONKE@USC-ISIB
YOUNGBERG@SRI-KA
ZEGERS@SRI-KL
ZOLOTOW@SRI-KL

ZOSEL@LLL-COMP

DIGITAL WILL BE GIVING A PRODUCT PRESENTATION OF THE NEWEST MEMBERS OF THE DECSYSTEM-20 FAMILY; THE DECSYSTEM-2020, 2020T, 2060, AND 2060T. THE DECSYSTEM-20 FAMILY OF COMPUTERS HAS EVOLVED FROM THE TENEX OPERATING SYSTEM AND THE DECSYSTEM-10 <PDP-10> COMPUTER ARCHITECTURE. BOTH THE DECSYSTEM-2060T AND 2020T OFFER FULL ARPANET SUPPORT UNDER THE TOPS-20 OPERATING SYSTEM.

THE DECSYSTEM-2060 IS AN UPWARD EXTENSION OF THE CURRENT DECSYSTEM-2040 AND 2050 FAMILY. THE DECSYSTEM-2020 IS A NEW LOW END MEMBER OF THE DECSYSTEM-20 FAMILY AND FULLY SOFTWARE COMPATIBLE WITH ALL OF THE OTHER DECSYSTEM-20 MODELS.

WE INVITE YOU TO COME SEE THE 2020 AND HEAR ABOUT THE DECSYSTEM-20 FAMILY AT THE TWO PRODUCT PRESENTATIONS WE WILL BE GIVING IN CALIFORNIA THIS MONTH. THE LOCATIONS WILL BE

TUESDAY, MAY 9, 1978 - 2 PM

The First Spam: The Email, Not The Meat

HYATT HOUSE (NEAR THE LA AIRPORT)
LOS ANGELES, CA

THURSDAY, MAY 11, 1978 - 2 PM
DUNFEY'S ROYAL COACH
SAN MATEO, CA
(4 MILES SOUTH OF S.F. AIRPORT AT BAYSHORE, RT 101
AND RT 92)

A 2020 WILL BE THERE FOR YOU TO VIEW ALSO TERMINALS ON-LINE TO OTHER
DECSYSTEM-20 SYSTEMS THROUGH THE ARPANET.

IF YOU ARE UNABLE TO ATTEND, PLEASE FEEL FREE TO
CONTACT THE NEAREST DEC OFFICE
FOR MORE INFORMATION ABOUT THE EXCITING
DECSYSTEM-20 FAMILY.

Below is one *response of a person who was forwarded this email Spam.*

Date: 10-MAY-78 23:20:30-PDT 2250;000000000001
Mail-from MIT-AI
rcvd at 7-MAY-78 2316-PDT
Date: 8 MAY 1978 0213-EDT
From RMS at MIT-AI (Richard M. Stallman)
Subject: MSGGROUP# 697 Some Thoughts about advertising
To: stefferud at USC-ISI
Redistributed-To: [ISI]<MsgGroup>Mailing.List;154:
Redistributed-By: STEFFERUD (connected to MSGGROUP)
Redistributed-Date: 8 MAY 1978

1) I didn't receive the DEC message, but I can't imagine I would have been bothered if I have. I get tons of uninteresting mail, and system announcements about babies born, etc. At least a demo MIGHT have been interesting.

The First Spam: The Email, Not The Meat

For more information about Lon Safko, please visit: www.Safko.com.

For more information about Gary Thuerk, please visit: https://www.linkedin.com/in/fatherespam

www.ingramcontent.com/pod-product-compliance
Lightning Source LLC
Chambersburg PA
CBHW050026230526
45470CB00003B/1152